50 Sizzling Summer Grills

By: Kelly Johnson

Table of Contents

- Grilled BBQ Ribs
- Classic Cheeseburgers
- Grilled Chicken Skewers
- Grilled Veggie Kebabs
- Marinated Flank Steak
- Grilled Shrimp Skewers
- Grilled Salmon Fillets
- Grilled Portobello Mushrooms
- Grilled Corn on the Cob
- Spicy Grilled Wings
- Grilled Lamb Chops
- Grilled Pineapple
- Grilled Fish Tacos
- Grilled Sausages
- Grilled Zucchini
- Grilled Chicken Caesar Salad
- Grilled Asparagus
- Grilled Veggie Tacos
- Grilled Pork Tenderloin
- Grilled Flatbreads
- Grilled Stuffed Peppers
- Grilled Shrimp and Vegetable Skewers
- Grilled Tomato Salad
- Grilled Avocado
- Grilled Caesar Salad
- BBQ Chicken Thighs
- Grilled Sweet Potatoes
- Grilled Eggplant
- Grilled Beef Burgers
- Grilled Scallops
- Grilled Sweet Corn Salad
- Grilled Lobster Tail
- Grilled Teriyaki Chicken
- Grilled Steak with Chimichurri Sauce
- Grilled Watermelon

- Grilled Marinated Tofu
- Grilled Halloumi Cheese
- Grilled Bone-In Ribeye
- Grilled Cajun Salmon
- Grilled Chicken Fajitas
- Grilled Caesar Veggie Wraps
- Grilled Bacon-Wrapped Shrimp
- Grilled Jerk Chicken
- Grilled Pizzas
- Grilled BBQ Pulled Pork Sandwiches
- Grilled Chili Lime Corn
- Grilled Fajita Vegetables
- Grilled Mushroom and Swiss Burgers
- Grilled Bacon-Wrapped Chicken
- Grilled Peaches with Honey

Grilled BBQ Ribs

Ingredients:

- 2 racks of baby back ribs
- 1/4 cup brown sugar
- 1/4 cup paprika
- 2 tbsp garlic powder
- 2 tbsp onion powder
- 1 tbsp ground black pepper
- 1 tbsp ground mustard
- 1 tsp ground cumin
- 1 tsp chili powder
- Salt to taste
- 1 cup BBQ sauce

Instructions:

1. **Prepare the Ribs:** Remove the membrane from the back of the ribs. Rinse and pat them dry with paper towels.
2. **Make the Rub:** In a bowl, combine brown sugar, paprika, garlic powder, onion powder, black pepper, mustard, cumin, chili powder, and salt.
3. **Season the Ribs:** Rub the seasoning mixture generously on both sides of the ribs.
4. **Grill the Ribs:** Preheat the grill to medium-low heat (about 250°F). Place the ribs on the grill over indirect heat and cook for 2.5-3 hours, flipping occasionally.
5. **Baste and Finish:** In the last 30 minutes of grilling, brush the ribs with BBQ sauce every 10 minutes until the ribs are tender and caramelized. Serve with extra BBQ sauce.

Classic Cheeseburgers

Ingredients:

- 1 lb ground beef (80% lean)
- Salt and pepper to taste
- 4 burger buns
- 4 slices of cheese (cheddar, American, or your preference)
- Lettuce, tomato, pickles, and onions for topping

Instructions:

1. **Form the Patties:** Divide the ground beef into 4 equal portions and shape them into patties. Season both sides with salt and pepper.
2. **Grill the Patties:** Preheat the grill to medium-high heat. Grill the patties for 4-5 minutes on each side, flipping once, until they reach desired doneness. Place cheese slices on the patties in the last minute of grilling to melt.
3. **Assemble the Burgers:** Toast the burger buns on the grill for about 1 minute. Place the cooked patties on the bottom buns, and top with lettuce, tomato, pickles, onions, and the top buns. Serve with your favorite condiments.

Grilled Chicken Skewers

Ingredients:

- 1 lb chicken breast, cut into bite-sized cubes
- 1/4 cup olive oil
- 1 tbsp lemon juice
- 2 cloves garlic, minced
- 1 tbsp dried oregano
- Salt and pepper to taste
- Wooden skewers (soaked in water for 30 minutes)

Instructions:

1. **Marinate the Chicken:** In a bowl, combine olive oil, lemon juice, garlic, oregano, salt, and pepper. Add the chicken cubes and mix until evenly coated. Let marinate for at least 30 minutes.
2. **Prepare the Skewers:** Thread the marinated chicken cubes onto the skewers.
3. **Grill the Skewers:** Preheat the grill to medium-high heat. Grill the chicken skewers for 4-5 minutes on each side, or until fully cooked and the internal temperature reaches 165°F.
4. **Serve:** Remove the skewers from the grill and serve with a side of rice or vegetables.

Grilled Veggie Kebabs

Ingredients:

- 1 zucchini, sliced into rounds
- 1 red bell pepper, cut into chunks
- 1 yellow bell pepper, cut into chunks
- 1 red onion, cut into chunks
- 8 oz mushrooms, whole or halved
- 1/4 cup olive oil
- 2 tbsp balsamic vinegar
- 2 tbsp fresh thyme or rosemary
- Salt and pepper to taste

Instructions:

1. **Prepare the Vegetables:** Thread the vegetables onto skewers, alternating between different types.
2. **Make the Marinade:** In a bowl, mix olive oil, balsamic vinegar, thyme, salt, and pepper.
3. **Marinate the Veggies:** Brush the vegetables with the marinade and let them sit for 15-20 minutes.
4. **Grill the Kebabs:** Preheat the grill to medium-high heat. Grill the veggie kebabs for about 4-5 minutes on each side until the vegetables are tender and slightly charred.
5. **Serve:** Serve the grilled veggie kebabs as a side dish or on their own with a drizzle of olive oil.

Marinated Flank Steak

Ingredients:

- 1 1/2 lbs flank steak
- 1/4 cup soy sauce
- 2 tbsp olive oil
- 2 tbsp balsamic vinegar
- 2 tbsp Dijon mustard
- 3 cloves garlic, minced
- 1 tbsp fresh rosemary, chopped
- Salt and pepper to taste

Instructions:

1. **Marinate the Steak:** In a bowl, whisk together soy sauce, olive oil, balsamic vinegar, mustard, garlic, rosemary, salt, and pepper. Place the flank steak in a zip-top bag or shallow dish and pour the marinade over the steak. Let marinate for at least 1 hour.
2. **Grill the Steak:** Preheat the grill to medium-high heat. Grill the flank steak for about 5-7 minutes per side for medium-rare, or longer for desired doneness.
3. **Rest and Slice:** Remove the steak from the grill and let it rest for 5-10 minutes. Slice against the grain and serve.

Grilled Shrimp Skewers

Ingredients:

- 1 lb large shrimp, peeled and deveined
- 2 tbsp olive oil
- 2 tbsp lemon juice
- 1 tsp smoked paprika
- 1 tsp garlic powder
- Salt and pepper to taste
- Wooden skewers (soaked in water for 30 minutes)

Instructions:

1. **Marinate the Shrimp:** In a bowl, combine olive oil, lemon juice, paprika, garlic powder, salt, and pepper. Toss the shrimp in the marinade and let them sit for 15-20 minutes.
2. **Prepare the Skewers:** Thread the shrimp onto the skewers.
3. **Grill the Shrimp:** Preheat the grill to medium-high heat. Grill the shrimp for 2-3 minutes on each side, until they are pink and opaque.
4. **Serve:** Remove the shrimp from the skewers and serve with a side of rice or a fresh salad.

Grilled Salmon Fillets

Ingredients:

- 4 salmon fillets (about 6 oz each)
- 2 tbsp olive oil
- 1 tbsp lemon juice
- 1 tsp garlic powder
- Salt and pepper to taste
- Fresh dill for garnish (optional)

Instructions:

1. **Prepare the Salmon:** Brush the salmon fillets with olive oil and lemon juice. Sprinkle with garlic powder, salt, and pepper.
2. **Grill the Salmon:** Preheat the grill to medium-high heat. Grill the salmon fillets for 4-6 minutes per side, until the flesh flakes easily with a fork.
3. **Serve:** Garnish with fresh dill and serve with a side of vegetables or potatoes.

Grilled Portobello Mushrooms

Ingredients:

- 4 large Portobello mushrooms, cleaned and stems removed
- 2 tbsp olive oil
- 1 tbsp balsamic vinegar
- 2 cloves garlic, minced
- Salt and pepper to taste
- Fresh parsley for garnish (optional)

Instructions:

1. **Marinate the Mushrooms:** In a bowl, whisk together olive oil, balsamic vinegar, garlic, salt, and pepper. Brush the mushrooms with the marinade and let them sit for 15-20 minutes.
2. **Grill the Mushrooms:** Preheat the grill to medium-high heat. Grill the mushrooms for 4-5 minutes per side, until tender and juicy.
3. **Serve:** Garnish with fresh parsley and serve as a side dish or on a bun as a vegetarian burger.

Grilled Corn on the Cob

Ingredients:

- 4 ears of corn, husked
- 2 tbsp olive oil or melted butter
- Salt and pepper to taste
- Optional: chili powder, paprika, or Parmesan cheese for seasoning

Instructions:

1. **Preheat the Grill:** Preheat the grill to medium heat.
2. **Prepare the Corn:** Brush the corn with olive oil or melted butter. Season with salt and pepper.
3. **Grill the Corn:** Place the corn directly on the grill. Grill for 10-15 minutes, turning occasionally, until the corn is tender and slightly charred.
4. **Serve:** Remove from the grill and season with additional spices or grated Parmesan cheese, if desired. Serve hot.

Spicy Grilled Wings

Ingredients:

- 12 chicken wings, separated into flats and drumettes
- 1/4 cup hot sauce
- 2 tbsp olive oil
- 1 tbsp smoked paprika
- 1 tsp cayenne pepper
- 1 tsp garlic powder
- Salt and pepper to taste

Instructions:

1. **Marinate the Wings:** In a bowl, mix hot sauce, olive oil, smoked paprika, cayenne, garlic powder, salt, and pepper. Toss the wings in the marinade and refrigerate for at least 1 hour.
2. **Grill the Wings:** Preheat the grill to medium-high heat. Grill the wings for 8-10 minutes per side, until crispy and cooked through.
3. **Serve:** Remove from the grill and serve with a side of ranch or blue cheese dressing and celery sticks.

Grilled Lamb Chops

Ingredients:

- 8 lamb chops
- 2 tbsp olive oil
- 2 tbsp fresh rosemary, chopped
- 3 cloves garlic, minced
- 1 tbsp lemon juice
- Salt and pepper to taste

Instructions:

1. **Marinate the Lamb:** In a bowl, mix olive oil, rosemary, garlic, lemon juice, salt, and pepper. Coat the lamb chops with the marinade and let sit for 30 minutes to 1 hour.
2. **Grill the Lamb:** Preheat the grill to medium-high heat. Grill the lamb chops for 3-4 minutes per side for medium-rare, or longer for desired doneness.
3. **Serve:** Let the lamb chops rest for a few minutes before serving. Garnish with additional rosemary if desired.

Grilled Pineapple

Ingredients:

- 1 pineapple, peeled, cored, and cut into rings or wedges
- 2 tbsp honey
- 1 tbsp lime juice
- Pinch of cinnamon (optional)

Instructions:

1. **Prepare the Pineapple:** Brush the pineapple slices with honey and lime juice, and sprinkle with a pinch of cinnamon, if using.
2. **Grill the Pineapple:** Preheat the grill to medium heat. Grill the pineapple for 2-3 minutes per side, until grill marks appear and the pineapple is caramelized.
3. **Serve:** Serve as a side dish, dessert, or over ice cream for a sweet treat.

Grilled Fish Tacos

Ingredients:

- 1 lb white fish fillets (tilapia, cod, or mahi-mahi)
- 2 tbsp olive oil
- 1 tbsp lime juice
- 1 tsp cumin
- Salt and pepper to taste
- Small corn tortillas
- Toppings: shredded cabbage, salsa, avocado, cilantro, lime wedges

Instructions:

1. **Marinate the Fish:** In a bowl, combine olive oil, lime juice, cumin, salt, and pepper. Coat the fish fillets in the marinade and let sit for 15-20 minutes.
2. **Grill the Fish:** Preheat the grill to medium heat. Grill the fish for 2-3 minutes per side, until cooked through and flaky.
3. **Assemble the Tacos:** Warm the tortillas on the grill. Flake the grilled fish and assemble the tacos with your favorite toppings, such as cabbage, salsa, avocado, cilantro, and lime.

Grilled Sausages

Ingredients:

- 4 sausages (your choice of flavor, such as bratwurst, Italian, or chorizo)
- 1 tbsp olive oil
- 1 onion, sliced (optional)
- 1 bell pepper, sliced (optional)

Instructions:

1. **Prepare the Grill:** Preheat the grill to medium heat.
2. **Grill the Sausages:** Place the sausages on the grill and cook for 6-8 minutes per side, turning occasionally, until fully cooked and browned.
3. **Optional:** While grilling the sausages, grill the onion and bell pepper slices in a grilling basket or on skewers.
4. **Serve:** Serve the sausages on buns with grilled vegetables or your favorite condiments.

Grilled Zucchini

Ingredients:

- 2 medium zucchinis, sliced into rounds or lengthwise
- 2 tbsp olive oil
- 1 tsp garlic powder
- Salt and pepper to taste
- Fresh parsley for garnish

Instructions:

1. **Prepare the Zucchini:** Brush the zucchini slices with olive oil and season with garlic powder, salt, and pepper.
2. **Grill the Zucchini:** Preheat the grill to medium-high heat. Grill the zucchini for 2-3 minutes per side, until tender and charred.
3. **Serve:** Garnish with fresh parsley and serve as a side dish.

Grilled Chicken Caesar Salad

Ingredients:

- 2 chicken breasts
- 2 tbsp olive oil
- Salt and pepper to taste
- 1 head of Romaine lettuce, halved lengthwise
- Caesar dressing
- Grated Parmesan cheese
- Croutons

Instructions:

1. **Grill the Chicken:** Preheat the grill to medium-high heat. Season the chicken breasts with olive oil, salt, and pepper. Grill the chicken for 5-6 minutes per side, until fully cooked. Let rest before slicing.
2. **Grill the Lettuce:** Brush the cut sides of the Romaine lettuce with olive oil and season with salt and pepper. Grill for 1-2 minutes per side, until slightly charred.
3. **Assemble the Salad:** Toss the grilled lettuce with Caesar dressing. Top with sliced grilled chicken, grated Parmesan, and croutons. Serve immediately.

Grilled Asparagus

Ingredients:

- 1 bunch of asparagus, trimmed
- 2 tbsp olive oil
- Salt and pepper to taste
- 1 tbsp lemon juice (optional)

Instructions:

1. **Prepare the Asparagus:** Drizzle the asparagus with olive oil and season with salt and pepper.
2. **Grill the Asparagus:** Preheat the grill to medium heat. Grill the asparagus for 3-4 minutes per side, until tender and lightly charred.
3. **Serve:** Drizzle with lemon juice, if desired, and serve as a side dish.

Grilled Veggie Tacos

Ingredients:

- 1 red bell pepper, sliced
- 1 zucchini, sliced
- 1 red onion, sliced
- 2 tbsp olive oil
- 1 tsp cumin
- 1 tsp chili powder
- Salt and pepper to taste
- Small flour or corn tortillas
- Toppings: salsa, avocado, cilantro, lime wedges

Instructions:

1. **Prepare the Veggies:** Toss the sliced bell pepper, zucchini, and onion in olive oil, cumin, chili powder, salt, and pepper.
2. **Grill the Veggies:** Preheat the grill to medium-high heat. Grill the veggies for 4-5 minutes per side until tender and lightly charred.
3. **Assemble the Tacos:** Warm the tortillas on the grill. Fill with grilled veggies and top with salsa, avocado, cilantro, and a squeeze of lime. Serve immediately.

Grilled Pork Tenderloin

Ingredients:

- 1 pork tenderloin (about 1 lb)
- 2 tbsp olive oil
- 1 tbsp honey
- 1 tbsp Dijon mustard
- 2 cloves garlic, minced
- 1 tsp thyme
- Salt and pepper to taste

Instructions:

1. **Marinate the Pork:** Mix olive oil, honey, Dijon mustard, garlic, thyme, salt, and pepper in a bowl. Coat the pork tenderloin with the marinade and refrigerate for at least 30 minutes.
2. **Grill the Pork:** Preheat the grill to medium-high heat. Grill the pork for 15-20 minutes, turning occasionally, until the internal temperature reaches 145°F (63°C).
3. **Serve:** Let the pork rest for a few minutes before slicing. Serve with your favorite sides.

Grilled Flatbreads

Ingredients:

- 2 flatbreads or naan
- 2 tbsp olive oil
- 1 tsp garlic powder
- 1 tsp dried oregano
- 1/2 cup crumbled feta or mozzarella cheese (optional)
- Fresh herbs for garnish (optional)

Instructions:

1. **Prepare the Flatbreads:** Brush the flatbreads with olive oil and sprinkle with garlic powder and oregano.
2. **Grill the Flatbreads:** Preheat the grill to medium heat. Grill the flatbreads for 2-3 minutes per side, until crispy and slightly charred.
3. **Top and Serve:** Optionally, sprinkle with cheese and fresh herbs before serving. Serve as an appetizer or side dish.

Grilled Stuffed Peppers

Ingredients:

- 4 bell peppers, tops cut off and seeds removed
- 1 cup cooked quinoa or rice
- 1 cup black beans, drained and rinsed
- 1/2 cup corn kernels
- 1 tsp cumin
- 1 tsp chili powder
- Salt and pepper to taste
- 1/2 cup shredded cheese (optional)

Instructions:

1. **Prepare the Stuffing:** In a bowl, combine the quinoa or rice, black beans, corn, cumin, chili powder, salt, and pepper.
2. **Stuff the Peppers:** Stuff each pepper with the quinoa mixture.
3. **Grill the Peppers:** Preheat the grill to medium heat. Place the stuffed peppers on the grill and cook for 10-15 minutes, until the peppers are tender. Top with cheese during the last few minutes of grilling, if desired.
4. **Serve:** Serve the stuffed peppers hot, garnished with fresh cilantro if desired.

Grilled Shrimp and Vegetable Skewers

Ingredients:

- 1 lb shrimp, peeled and deveined
- 1 red bell pepper, cut into chunks
- 1 zucchini, sliced into rounds
- 1 red onion, cut into chunks
- 2 tbsp olive oil
- 1 tbsp lemon juice
- 1 tsp paprika
- Salt and pepper to taste

Instructions:

1. **Prepare the Skewers:** In a bowl, toss the shrimp and vegetables with olive oil, lemon juice, paprika, salt, and pepper.
2. **Assemble the Skewers:** Thread the shrimp and vegetables onto skewers, alternating between shrimp and veggies.
3. **Grill the Skewers:** Preheat the grill to medium-high heat. Grill the skewers for 2-3 minutes per side, until the shrimp are pink and cooked through.
4. **Serve:** Remove the skewers from the grill and serve immediately with a side of rice or salad.

Grilled Tomato Salad

Ingredients:

- 4 large tomatoes, halved
- 2 tbsp olive oil
- 1 tsp balsamic vinegar
- Salt and pepper to taste
- Fresh basil for garnish

Instructions:

1. **Prepare the Tomatoes:** Brush the tomato halves with olive oil and season with salt and pepper.
2. **Grill the Tomatoes:** Preheat the grill to medium heat. Grill the tomatoes for 2-3 minutes per side, until lightly charred.
3. **Make the Salad:** Drizzle the grilled tomatoes with balsamic vinegar and garnish with fresh basil. Serve warm or at room temperature.

Grilled Avocado

Ingredients:

- 2 ripe avocados, halved and pitted
- 1 tbsp olive oil
- Salt and pepper to taste
- Optional toppings: lime juice, cilantro, or crumbled feta

Instructions:

1. **Prepare the Avocados:** Brush the avocado halves with olive oil and season with salt and pepper.
2. **Grill the Avocados:** Preheat the grill to medium-high heat. Grill the avocado halves for 2-3 minutes, until grill marks appear and they are warmed through.
3. **Serve:** Top with lime juice, cilantro, or crumbled feta, and serve as a side dish or appetizer.

Grilled Caesar Salad

Ingredients:

- 1 head of Romaine lettuce, halved
- 2 tbsp olive oil
- Salt and pepper to taste
- Caesar dressing
- Grated Parmesan cheese
- Croutons

Instructions:

1. **Prepare the Lettuce:** Brush the cut sides of the Romaine lettuce with olive oil and season with salt and pepper.
2. **Grill the Lettuce:** Preheat the grill to medium heat. Grill the lettuce for 1-2 minutes per side, until slightly charred.
3. **Assemble the Salad:** Drizzle the grilled lettuce with Caesar dressing, then top with grated Parmesan and croutons. Serve immediately.

BBQ Chicken Thighs

Ingredients:

- 8 bone-in, skin-on chicken thighs
- 1/2 cup BBQ sauce
- Salt and pepper to taste

Instructions:

1. **Prepare the Chicken:** Season the chicken thighs with salt and pepper. Brush with BBQ sauce.
2. **Grill the Chicken:** Preheat the grill to medium heat. Grill the chicken thighs for 6-8 minutes per side, until the internal temperature reaches 165°F (74°C).
3. **Serve:** Let the chicken rest for a few minutes before serving. Serve with extra BBQ sauce on the side.

Grilled Sweet Potatoes

Ingredients:

- 2 large sweet potatoes, peeled and cut into 1-inch thick rounds
- 2 tbsp olive oil
- 1 tsp paprika
- 1 tsp garlic powder
- Salt and pepper to taste

Instructions:

1. **Prepare the Sweet Potatoes:** Toss the sweet potato rounds in olive oil, paprika, garlic powder, salt, and pepper.
2. **Grill the Sweet Potatoes:** Preheat the grill to medium heat. Grill the sweet potato slices for 3-4 minutes per side until tender and lightly charred.
3. **Serve:** Serve hot with a sprinkle of fresh herbs, if desired.

Grilled Eggplant

Ingredients:

- 2 medium eggplants, sliced into 1/2-inch thick rounds
- 3 tbsp olive oil
- 1 tsp dried oregano
- Salt and pepper to taste

Instructions:

1. **Prepare the Eggplant:** Brush the eggplant slices with olive oil and sprinkle with oregano, salt, and pepper.
2. **Grill the Eggplant:** Preheat the grill to medium-high heat. Grill the eggplant for 3-4 minutes per side until tender and grill marks appear.
3. **Serve:** Serve immediately, optionally topped with crumbled feta or a drizzle of balsamic glaze.

Grilled Beef Burgers

Ingredients:

- 1 lb ground beef (80% lean)
- Salt and pepper to taste
- 4 burger buns
- Toppings: lettuce, tomato, cheese, pickles, ketchup, mustard

Instructions:

1. **Prepare the Patties:** Form the ground beef into 4 equal-sized patties. Season with salt and pepper on both sides.
2. **Grill the Burgers:** Preheat the grill to medium-high heat. Grill the patties for 4-5 minutes per side for medium doneness.
3. **Serve:** Toast the buns on the grill. Assemble the burgers with your favorite toppings and serve immediately.

Grilled Scallops

Ingredients:

- 12 large sea scallops, patted dry
- 2 tbsp olive oil
- 1 tsp lemon zest
- Salt and pepper to taste
- Fresh parsley for garnish

Instructions:

1. **Prepare the Scallops:** Drizzle the scallops with olive oil and season with lemon zest, salt, and pepper.
2. **Grill the Scallops:** Preheat the grill to medium-high heat. Grill the scallops for 2-3 minutes per side, until opaque and slightly caramelized.
3. **Serve:** Garnish with fresh parsley and a squeeze of lemon juice before serving.

Grilled Sweet Corn Salad

Ingredients:

- 4 ears of corn, husked
- 1 red bell pepper, diced
- 1/4 cup red onion, finely diced
- 1/4 cup cilantro, chopped
- 2 tbsp lime juice
- 1 tbsp olive oil
- Salt and pepper to taste

Instructions:

1. **Grill the Corn:** Preheat the grill to medium heat. Grill the corn for 8-10 minutes, turning occasionally, until charred and tender. Let cool slightly before cutting off the kernels.
2. **Prepare the Salad:** In a bowl, combine the grilled corn kernels, bell pepper, onion, and cilantro. Drizzle with lime juice and olive oil, then season with salt and pepper.
3. **Serve:** Serve chilled or at room temperature as a refreshing side dish.

Grilled Lobster Tail

Ingredients:

- 4 lobster tails
- 3 tbsp melted butter
- 1 tbsp lemon juice
- 1 tsp paprika
- Salt and pepper to taste

Instructions:

1. **Prepare the Lobster Tails:** Cut the lobster tails in half lengthwise, brushing the meat with melted butter, lemon juice, paprika, salt, and pepper.
2. **Grill the Lobster:** Preheat the grill to medium-high heat. Grill the lobster tails, flesh side down, for 5-7 minutes until the meat is opaque and slightly charred.
3. **Serve:** Serve immediately with extra lemon wedges and melted butter for dipping.

Grilled Teriyaki Chicken

Ingredients:

- 4 chicken breasts
- 1/4 cup soy sauce
- 2 tbsp honey
- 1 tbsp rice vinegar
- 1 clove garlic, minced
- 1 tsp ginger, grated
- 1 tbsp sesame seeds (optional)

Instructions:

1. **Marinate the Chicken:** In a bowl, whisk together the soy sauce, honey, rice vinegar, garlic, and ginger. Marinate the chicken breasts in this mixture for at least 30 minutes.
2. **Grill the Chicken:** Preheat the grill to medium-high heat. Grill the chicken for 6-7 minutes per side until the internal temperature reaches 165°F (74°C).
3. **Serve:** Garnish with sesame seeds and serve with a side of steamed rice or veggies.

Grilled Steak with Chimichurri Sauce

Ingredients:

- 2 ribeye steaks or your preferred cut
- Salt and pepper to taste
- 1/2 cup fresh parsley, chopped
- 2 tbsp red wine vinegar
- 3 tbsp olive oil

- 2 garlic cloves, minced
- 1/2 tsp red pepper flakes (optional)

Instructions:

1. **Grill the Steaks:** Preheat the grill to medium-high heat. Season the steaks with salt and pepper. Grill for 4-5 minutes per side for medium-rare or longer for your desired doneness.
2. **Prepare the Chimichurri Sauce:** In a bowl, combine the parsley, red wine vinegar, olive oil, garlic, and red pepper flakes. Stir to combine.
3. **Serve:** Let the steaks rest for a few minutes, then slice and serve with chimichurri sauce drizzled on top.

www.ingramcontent.com/pod-product-compliance
Lightning Source LLC
LaVergne TN
LVHW060332080526
838201LV00118BA/3040